W9-BRN-441

WHAT ARE TAXES?

LYNNAE D. STEINBERG

Britannica®
Educational Publishing

IN ASSOCIATION WITH

ROSEN
EDUCATIONAL SERVICES

Published in 2016 by Britannica Educational Publishing (a trademark of Encyclopædia Britannica, Inc.) in association with The Rosen Publishing Group, Inc.
29 East 21st Street, New York, NY 10010

Distributed exclusively by Rosen Publishing.
To see additional Britannica Educational Publishing titles, go to rosenpublishing.com.

First Edition

Britannica Educational Publishing
J. E. Luebering: Director, Core Reference Group
Mary Rose McCudden: Editor, Britannica Student Encyclopedia

Rosen Publishing
John Kemmerer: Executive Editor
Jacob R. Steinberg: Editor
Nelson Sá: Art Director
Danijah Brevard: Designer
Cindy Reiman: Photography Manager

Library of Congress Cataloging-in-Publication Data

Steinberg, Lynnae D., 1957–
What are taxes?/Lynnae D. Steinberg. — First Edition.
     pages cm. — (Let's find out! Government)
Includes bibliographical references and index.
ISBN 978-1-62275-981-1 (library bound) — ISBN 978-1-62275-982-8 (pbk.) — ISBN 978-1-62275-984-2 (6-pack)
1. Taxation — United States — Juvenile literature. 2. Taxation — Juvenile literature. I. Title.
HJ2381.S74 2016
336.200973 — dc23
                                                                2014037269

Manufactured in the United States of America

CONTENTS

WHAT ARE TAXES?

You've had your eye on something special at the store for a while. Today, you're finally ready to buy it. The store clerk asks for the money, but it's more than the amount on the price tag! Why does it cost more than it says? The answer is taxes.

Governments can collect money in different ways. State governments sell license plates for cars and other

Shoppers must keep taxes in mind when choosing items to buy.

automobiles. They also charge fees for driver's licenses. City governments can ask you to pay for licenses to get married or to own a pet. Sometimes they even charge money to park your car on certain streets.

Almost every government gets money by taking a certain amount from its citizens. This money is called a tax. The more that you know about taxes and how they work, the better you will be at managing and saving your own money.

EARLY FORMS OF TAXES

Many ancient farmers, such as the one in this Egyptian painting, had to give a portion of their crops to the government as payment.

In ancient times, people sometimes gave goods or services to support their governments. One of the oldest types of taxes was for land and crops. It was called a tithe. A tithe was one-tenth of a farmer's crops or the animals he raised.

Imagine life in ancient times. Some people own little land, so they don't grow many crops. Others own a lot of land and grow more crops. Why is a tithe a fair way of collecting taxes?

Another ancient tax was called the corvée (pronounced "kor-VAY"). The corvée was a type of unpaid work that poor people could do for a short time if they couldn't afford to give their government crops or money. Some people might have had to help build a road or a bridge. Some citizens might have been sent to fight in a battle. These people helped the government for a short time and then went back to normal life.

Many believe that the ancient Egyptian pyramids were built not by slaves but by workers who owed service to the rulers.

Taxes in Ancient Rome

In ancient Rome the government collected taxes in the form of money. The Romans taxed people in many different ways. One tax—called a head tax—was an equal amount that every citizen had to pay. Paying taxes was hard for some people, but the Roman government used these taxes to support its empire.

 The Romans built 50,000 miles (80,467 km) of hard-surfaced roads, many of which still exist today!

Aqueducts, such as this one, had channels on top of them that carried water over long distances.

One way the Romans used taxes was to build roads and bridges. Their road system made it easier to trade with far-off lands. It also made it easier to spread news throughout the empire.

Roman city planners also used taxes to build aqueducts, or water pipes. Aqueducts made it easier for people to get fresh, clean water. They also carried away dirty water that had unhealthy germs in it. The Roman government used taxes to make people's lives better.

COMPARE AND CONTRAST

How is the head tax different from a tithe? Why might a head tax be harder on poorer people than a tithe?

No Taxation Without Representation

This map from 1758 shows some of the 13 American colonies, which were under British rule.

Over the years, taxes became more important. Governments counted on taxes as a source of money. However, people sometimes have been unhappy with the taxes they have to pay. One example of this was the people in the American colonies more than 200 years ago.

The people who founded the colonies had left England

The British Parliament, depicted here, made the laws that American colonists had to follow.

to start a new life. They wanted the freedom to make choices about how they lived. Before the 1760s, the American colonies had a lot of freedom.

However, they were still colonies of Great Britain, and the British government ruled over them.

In 1765, the British Parliament forced the colonies to pay new taxes. The Parliament was the group that made laws in Great Britain. The American colonists thought Parliament was not treating them fairly. The colonists had to pay taxes to Great Britain, but there was no one in Parliament to represent them or to speak for them. The colonists called this "taxation without representation."

It Started with the Stamp Act!

In 1765, members of Parliament passed a law called the Stamp Act. It said colonists had to put a stamp on printed items such as legal papers and newspapers. They had to buy this stamp from the British government. The Stamp Act made the colonists angry. They refused to buy the stamps.

Representatives from nine colonies had a meeting. They wrote a list of the reasons why they didn't like the tax. They asked the British government to take back the law. Merchants in the colonies

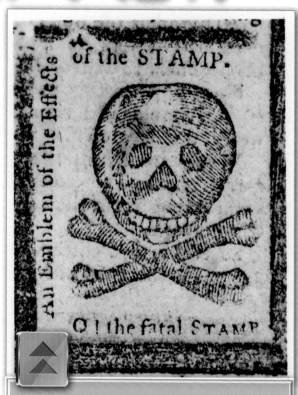

This picture of a stamp with a skull on it was made to show that the colonists did not like the Stamp Act.

also agreed not to buy items from Great Britain. That meant people in Great Britain could not sell things they made to people in the colonies. Great Britain lost money.

Because of the protests, the British Parliament ended the tax in 1766. The Stamp Act had helped bring the colonists together. It also led to some of the first protests by American colonists against the British government.

Colonists gathered together to protest the Stamp Act and to burn items that had the stamp!

THINK ABOUT IT

What are some reasons the colonists might have been in favor of protesting, or not buying, certain goods from Great Britain? Why could they have been against protesting British goods?

The Townshend Acts

NOTHING WAS THOUGHT OF BUT THIS TAXATION,
AND THE EASIEST METHOD OF LIQUIDATION.

T-A-X

'TWAS ENOUGH TO VEX
THE SOULS OF THE MEN OF BOSTON TOWN,
TO READ THIS UNDER THE SEAL OF THE CROWN.

TAX·ON·
TEA·
3d per lb

1773

THEY WERE LOYAL SUBJECTS OF GEORGE THE THIRD;
SO THEY ... D AND SO THEY AVERRED,
UT THIS ... G, OFFENSIVE PLACARD SET
ON THE ... AS WORSE THAN A BAYONET,

After the Stamp Act was ended, a British official named Charles Townshend got Parliament to pass several new tax laws. The Townshend Acts were four laws that angered the colonists even more. One of the acts taxed tea, lead, paint, paper, and glass coming into colonial ports. These products were important for helping to

The Townshend Acts of 1767 included an unpopular tax on tea.

build new homes, towns, and businesses in the colonies. Furthermore, the colonists still did not have representation in Parliament.

One of the Townshend Acts even let British spies check to make sure colonists paid the taxes! To keep order, the British government sent soldiers to Boston, Massachusetts, in 1768. On March 5, 1770, a group of British soldiers tried to calm down angry colonists. The colonists were shouting and threw things at the soldiers. The soldiers shot their guns at the crowd. Five colonists were killed. This event was known as the Boston Massacre. It made colonists speak out against rule by Britain.

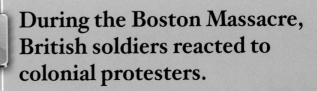

During the Boston Massacre, British soldiers reacted to colonial protesters.

"UNITED WE STAND"

On the same day as the Boston Massacre, Parliament did away with most of the Townshend Acts. They kept the tax on tea, however. Then, in 1773, Parliament passed the Tea Act, which allowed a British company to sell tea at a lower price than American companies. On December 16, 1773, American colonists boarded British ships in Boston Harbor. They threw the British tea into the water to protest the taxes. This event became known as the Boston Tea Party.

English tea chests were tossed overboard by colonists dressed as Native Americans.

The British government passed new laws. The colonists called them the Intolerable Acts. They were a punishment for the Boston Tea Party. The laws said the colonists had to pay for the tea they ruined. The 13 American colonies decided to work together. They thought the British government was not treating them fairly. Because of that, they wanted to be free from British rule. The British taxes and the Boston Tea Party led to the American Revolution!

On June 28, 1776, the Declaration of Independence was signed, an important event during the American Revolution.

WHY DO WE HAVE TAXES?

Taxes are the money that a government collects from the people who live in a city, state, or country. The government uses that money to pay for what it needs.

Governments collect taxes for many reasons. The most important one is to pay for services. One example of these services is an army or police officers to protect

Drivers can see their tax dollars at work as roads are repaired with government funds.

THINK ABOUT IT

Do you think it is fair for a government to make people pay more because of their personal behavior? Why or why not?

people. Another example of government services is building roads and bridges—as the ancient Romans did.

Some governments use taxes to try to change people's behavior. For example, they may put high taxes on cigarettes to help people stop smoking. Many states have used taxes to try and make people avoid unhealthy food or soda. Businesses sometimes pay higher taxes if the products they make are unhealthy in some way.

Some governments hope that higher taxes on sugary drinks will convince citizens to make healthier choices at the supermarket.

INCOME TAXES

In the United States almost everyone who works pays some type of tax. That is because people pay taxes on the money they earn at their jobs. This type of tax is called an income tax. A tax on the money that people make is called a personal income tax. Businesses also pay taxes on the money they make. They pay a corporate income tax.

> **VOCABULARY**
> Any of the money that somebody earns from work, business, or his or her property is called **income**.

Companies in the United States often take some of a worker's income and send the money straight to the government. Income tax

Form **1040**
For the year Jan. 1–Dec. 31, 2013, or other tax year beginning
Department of the Treasury—Internal Revenue
U.S. Individual Income Tax
Your first name and initial

◀◀ In the United States, income tax forms and payments are due each year on April 15.

The Internal Revenue Service headquarters is located in Washington, D.C.

is used to help pay for national services such as the mail. Some states also collect their own tax on income.

The more money you earn, the more taxes you must pay. The Internal Revenue Service (IRS) is the agency that is in charge of taxes. Every year it collects income taxes from American workers. In the United States the first income tax started in 1862 during the American Civil War.

WHAT'S IMPORTANT IN YOUR TOWN?

Many states, counties, and towns collect their own taxes, too. These taxes help pay for programs that help the people who live in those communities. Some state taxes pay for health care. This helps pay for people who can't afford to see the doctor or buy medicine on their own. State governments collect the taxes from

Medicaid is a health insurance program funded by taxes and managed by individual states.

everybody. Then they give some of the money to those people who need it.

Local taxes can also be used to give money to schools. In every community there are public schools that children can go to for free. Public schools are usually supported by state, county, and local taxes. If the citizens in a county or state care about having good schools, they can vote for more taxes that will pay for better schools.

The first public school in the United States (pictured here) was opened in Boston in 1635.

THINK ABOUT IT

Schools are just one part of your community paid for by local taxes. What other places or services in your town can you think of that town or county taxes might help pay for?

More at the Checkout!

Sales tax is an extra tax when people buy certain goods and services. Another name for this type of tax is value-added tax (VAT). Some products may be exempt from sales tax, which means they are not taxed. They are usually basic needs, such as food and education.

In the United States, sales tax is often added to the price of something when you pay for it. That is why some

The amount of money that you paid for tax on an item you bought can be found on your receipt.

things cost more than the amount on the price tag. In Europe, countries include the VAT in the price of the item. All people pay the same amount of sales tax on an item. As prices go up, taxes may also increase.

Sales taxes can be set aside for special purposes. For example, taxes from the gas people put in their cars are often used to pay for fixing roads or for public transportation.

When your parents fill up the car with gas, they might pay taxes that pay for such services as fixing roads.

THINK ABOUT IT
Around the beginning of the new school year, many states offer a tax-free week to help make certain school products cheaper to buy. What supplies do you think make the most sense to be tax-free and why?

What Is a Tariff?

Tariffs are special taxes collected only on products that go from one country to another. They are also called duties or customs. The most common kind of tariff is an import tariff. An import tariff is a tax on **foreign** businesses that want to sell their goods in a country. An export tariff

Container ships transport goods in and out of the United States' ports, where they are often taxed.

is a tax on a country's own businesses. Companies must pay the government before sending their goods out of the country to sell. Transit tariffs are taxes on goods passing through one country on their way to another country.

Tariffs have existed since the Middle Ages. Countries often charge higher tariffs during hard times, such as war. When the economy is good, tariffs become less common. Some countries have agreements with each other not to collect tariffs. These deals increase trade.

VOCABULARY

When something is considered **foreign**, it means it comes from somewhere outside of our own country.

Raising Money Without Taxes

In the 1900s, some governments looked for ways to collect money without adding or raising taxes. Many began using lotteries. A lottery is a gambling game. A large number of people buy tickets in hopes of winning a prize. The prizes might be goods or some of the money raised. Sometimes the money raised in a lottery is used for special projects. Lotteries are different from taxes because nobody is required to participate.

Many states use lotteries to fund such things as education.

COMPARE AND CONTRAST
What are some ways that lotteries and taxes are similar? How are they different?

There are many ways governments collect the money they need, but taxes are the most common. Some taxes are different for each person (such as income taxes). Other taxes are the same for everyone (sales taxes). Different people think different kinds of taxes are good or bad. Being aware of how your government collects and uses taxes will help you to become a successful and responsible citizen.

ODCT "Keeping Oregon on the Move"

YOUR TAX DOLLARS AT WORK

COMPLETION FALL 2009

Taxes in the United States are used in many ways to improve the lives of citizens!

GLOSSARY

ancient Relating to a time early in history.

citizens The people who are full members of a country, state, or town.

colonies A group of people from one country who live in a new territory but keep ties with the parent state.

customs Another name for taxes paid on imports or exports.

duties Another name for taxes paid on imports or exports.

empire A large territory or a number of territories or peoples, under a single authority.

exempt Free from a requirement to which others are subject.

gambling Relating to games where one bets on an uncertain outcome.

government The people, laws, and customs that rule over a country.

income Money earned from work, business, or property owned.

massacre The killing of a number of helpless human beings.

merchant A buyer and seller of goods.

Middle Ages The period of European history from about 500 CE to 1500.

ports Harbor towns or cities where ships load or unload cargo.

protest To object or show some type of disagreement.

services Useful work or groups that provide for some type of public need.

value The amount of money that something is worth.

For More Information

Books

Brennan, Linda Crotta. *Taxes* (Simple Economics). North Mankato, MN: Child's World, 2012.

De Capua, Sarah. *Paying Taxes.* New York, NY: Children's Press (Scholastic), 2012.

Gondosch, Linda. *How Did Tea and Taxes Spark a Revolution?* Minneapolis, MN: Lerner Classroom, 2010.

Harmon, Julian. *My Dad Pays Taxes.* New York, NY: Rosen Publishing, 2013.

Websites

Because of the changing nature of Internet links, Rosen Publishing has developed an online list of websites related to the subject of this book. This site is updated regularly. Please use this link to access this list:

http://www.rosenlinks.com/LFO/Tax

INDEX